BARBARA I. AUS

MW00941257

The Essential Curriculum

21 ideas for developing a positive and optimistic culture

WWW.AWAKENINGSCHOOLS.COM

Copyright © 2013 Barbara I. Aust B.Ed., M.Ed.
All rights reserved.
ISBN: 1489532684
ISBN 13: 9781489532688
Library of Congress Control Number: 2013910107
CreateSpace Independent Publishing Platform
North Charleston, South Carolina

Dedicated

*to my precious grandchildren who teach me so much
about unconditional love*

essentialcurriculum, ca

Gratitude

*Each of us has cause
to think with deep gratitude
of those who have lighted
the flame within us.*

—Albert Schweitzer

There are so many people who have provided me with fertile soil in which to grow. To each and every one of you I extend my heartfelt appreciation.

My late parents demonstrated the virtues of caring, dedication, and service by looking after the generations that came before them. Growing up in a four-generation house was certainly a place to observe the golden thread of life. My aunt, uncle, sister-cousin, and four siblings were a large part of that upbringing, and to all of you I owe a great deal.

My husband of more than four decades has always been able to make me laugh when I take life too seriously. You have taught me much about the virtues of courage and independence.

My children and their spouses have added richness to my life. You have encouraged me to have heart and compassion, to be patient, and to live in gratitude for whatever life brings. My grandchildren have taught me about unconditional love. Because of you my eyes are more fully open to beauty, awe, and wonder.

Two remarkable women hold special places in my heart: my aunt, Jean Levis, and the late Sandra Hohlachoff. You kept me afloat in the early days and I will be forever grateful.

The great university of life has provided me with faithful friends who have been pivotal in my world. You have taught me how to be in relationship with others, and our unity in spirit is something to be treasured. Many of you have been "angels in disguise" and at significant times have provided sparks to rekindle my inner flame. Namaste.

Educators, students, and parents the world over have enriched my professional life. I am grateful for the privilege I have had in working with you to try to create a better world, especially the years with one amazing teacher, "my pard," Wendy Vine.

Last, but certainly not least, is my wonderful guide, the late Sydney Banks. What a path you led me to!

You have all been wonderful teachers for me, and I will be forever grateful.

Preamble

This little book emerged when I temporarily came out of retirement and assumed a principalship to cover a sick leave.

As I sat once again at the big desk, surprised to be back doing something I had left a couple of years before, I wondered what I could do that might be helpful to a new person coming into this role.

That afternoon of contemplation led me to write a journal at the end of each day, to take the events that arose and turn them into lessons for someone who would be new to the administrative chair.

Each afternoon, I met with my "imaginary new administrator" and wrote the lesson of the day. Over the course of eight months, I wrote an entire book that distilled into a month's worth of lessons for a person new to working with students, staff, and parents. Upon reflection, I discovered that it had relevance in all situations, not just those in a school. Names, locations and actual events have often been altered to respect privacy. The stories come from a long career that has taken on many forms in a number of different locales.

Each lesson is brief and contains a simple but important message. These lessons may seem repetitive, with a similar theme running through them, but there are only so many ways to say "it's all about love" and "it's important to treat others the way you would like to be treated." The world's major religions have found a way to say this in a single sentence!

Baha'i: …choose thou for thy neighbor that which thou choosest for thyself.

Buddhism: Hurt not others in ways that you yourself would find hurtful.

Christianity: All things whatsoever that ye would that men should do unto you, do ye even so unto them.

Hinduism: Do not unto others what would cause pain unto you.

Islam: No one of you is a believer until he desires for his brother that which he desires for himself.

Judaism: What is hateful to you do not do to others.

Taoism: Regard your neighbors' gain as your own gain and your neighbors' loss as your own loss.

This little book has a similar message but in twenty-one excerpts. Read one a day and reflect on what it might mean in your context. Allow it to percolate and be assimilated into your way of thinking.

I hope that it is helpful to you and piques your interest enough that you will want to explore the source materials further. Above all, I hope you go away from reading this with these three possibilities in mind:

- *Change is possible.*

- *There are no "throwaway" people.*

- *The essence of success lies in nurturing positive, genuine feelings and recognizing the virtues in one another.*

I wish you the best of luck and much joy as you work with the youth of the world.

Barb Aust,

British Columbia, Canada

~ 1 ~
Change is Possible

Invite people to the table

"You get the best effort from others not by lighting a fire beneath them but by building a fire within."
Bob Nelson, author and motivational speaker, USA

When we invite people to join us at the table, we come as equals. It blurs the lines to provide a more neutral place for all to engage in the process of developing rapport and successful communication. Staff, parents, and students become participants in learning and not merely recipients of the ideas of others. The atmosphere becomes generative, welcoming, and encouraging.

Invitational learning offers room for choice. The dialogue invites participation, the feeling is welcoming, and the door is open. This is a place where passion is acknowledged, where people can be who they are without judgment.

I noticed that as the demands of the external bureaucracies increased, there was a tendency to forget what I had learned about the most effective way for young people to learn. It became increasingly challenging to find ways to support learning as it became more prescriptive.

I had to remind myself that the essential curriculum is the underpinning of all other learning—that without a belief in possibility, seeing the potential in everyone and experiencing it surrounded by an essence of positive and optimistic feelings, no bureaucratic decree would make things better.

I encouraged my staffs to be creative, sometimes even subversive! They were encouraged to make sure that all the i's were dotted and t's crossed so that we were being honest in our commitment to the ministry of education, yet at the same time I encouraged them to find ways to educate students in a way that was enjoyable and fostered sustainable learning.

If the three prescribed learning principles in our province were followed, we could not go wrong. These learning principles state that children learn in a variety of ways and at different rates, learning is an individual and group process, and students need to be active participants in their learning. Underpin that with the essential curriculum and all will be well.

When students have the opportunity to "show how they know," they are empowered to come from their place of comfort, excellence, and passion. They can then expand their zone of proximal development as they gain confidence. It provides an opportunity for students to feel empowered in their learning.

Participants come to the table with more clarity and the ability to access their wisdom when we are invitational. Contributions can be made from more open places, and the chance for clear, clean, and insightful decision making is enhanced.

Rely on common sense and wisdom

"Meditate and seek peace, for it is in the silent chambers of your mind that you will uncover the wisdom you seek."
Sydney Banks, author, philosopher and theosophist

This modern era of swift communication is beneficial because it can get us information quickly, but it can also be a nightmare!

One of my colleagues found this out in a most humbling fashion. Joelle reacted from anger and frustration and, in that moment, lost sight of the fact that her own mood had plummeted. The action she took was from her lower feeling state, where the "monkey chatter" in her brain kept saying, "The guy is a $@&% and I am going to show him!"

Joelle typed the most scathing e-mail imaginable. She went back to an old way of thinking that told her if she could get her anger out she would feel a whole lot better. You probably know where this story is going—and yes, she did! Joelle pushed SEND instead of SAVE, both words that start in S but with such different meanings!

Now in the old days, you could write that letter and later tear it up or burn it, but in today's world where we simply push a button, devastating results can be what comes rather than a little pile of ash. Ashes for sure, but not the ashes she was counting on!

Joelle received a phone call the following day from a very upset parent who informed her that she had notified the principal, the superintendent, the school board, and the minister of education about her behavior. Needless to say, Joelle had to mend many fences over the next few months and in fact moved to a new school district, hoping that her reputation for anger issues did not follow her. Had Joelle remembered that a calm and quiet mind is the greatest asset one can have when you need to solve a problem quickly and efficiently, things may have turned out differently. Allowing anger to get the best of her, Joelle moved away from her common sense, and it led her down a destructive path. Had Joelle been open to slowing down her mind and letting go of the negative thoughts that were cluttering her brain, she would have been able to be receptive to her own common sense and wisdom.

Listening to ourselves in a detached and neutral fashion can be very enlightening. It provides us with a hint at how mind, thought, and consciousness work together to create our reality.

Awareness of our moods and feelings is an indicator of our level of consciousness at any given moment. If we are in a low mood, we see the world through dark-colored glasses. If we are brave enough to listen to ourselves from a detached and neutral place when feeling low, we have the opportunity to hear our biases and judgments. Sometimes it comes as a big surprise, but always it gives us the opportunity to change.

As our mood goes up, the thoughts change and we view the world from an entirely different perspective. It almost seems like magic—one moment the world looks bleak, and the next it can take on the most beautiful hue imaginable.

What is the difference? Our thinking has changed and, along with it, our perception of the world around us.

Anyone who has ever worked with students has experienced what happens with a change in his or her level of consciousness. One minute a student can be making you tear your hair out because you simply can't seem to get anything from them. Yet moments or days later, something changes and you are able to see that same student with a fresh set of eyes and a new perspective. Suddenly, everything appears different. The only thing that has really changed is your viewing place.

It is such a simple thing, and as long as we don't become gripped by what appears before our eyes, we'll remember that appearances can be deceiving! We need to remember to be mindful and to be aware of our "come from"—our personal perspective.

Be patient and find your place of calmness

"Only in quiet waters do things mirror themselves undistorted. Only in a quiet mind is adequate perception of the world."
Hans Margolius, author on ethics

Usually anything can be solved with patience, understanding, and a calm mind. When problems arise, there can be a heightened state of angst or insecurity. This is not the time or space in which to resolve an issue. Our thoughts, and subsequently our actions, respond to our state of mind. When feeling fear and insecurity, our thinking is clouded, and we respond from a lower level of understanding.

When we slow down the mind chatter, settle down, and get centered, a calmer state of mind comes to the surface. A wonderful colleague taught me a valuable lesson on this topic. I was frustrated by the slow response of certain people in staff meetings. Ricardo responded, "Just remember the ten-second pause." "Pardon?" I said. "I don't know what you are talking about." Ricardo went on to explain that I needed to learn some patience. He reminded me that not everyone can respond quickly and that if I just slowed it down a little and waited, an answer would come.

This insight turned out to have huge benefits over the years both for those I was working with and for me. I learned to wait for others to give an answer, including the students in my class. I counted to ten in my head when waiting for an answer from particular students. When asking people to try something new, I would give them time to assimilate the information before engaging in a conversation. But best of all, and selfishly I might add, I learned to say, "Let me think about that for a while and I will get back to you." This meant I didn't have to live in a heightened state of readiness at every second. Talk about a stress reliever!

This also works when there is a conflict. Conflicts do arise and, handled from a space that is calm and neutral, can be resolved more easily. When we are able to speak from a place of non judgment and keep our voices down to deescalate the feelings of angst, a more level playing field emerges. When the person mediating the conflict is able to remain calm, the issue can be discussed and dealt with, minus the heightened state of emotion.

Without doubt, people need to be held to account, but increased angst and hostile feelings are not the direction to go in. Messing around in the "he said, she said" details does not solve problems; they are resolved by choosing to get back to a good feeling.

So we need to be aware of our feelings. If the feelings are positive and the atmosphere is calm, thoughts will be correspondingly uplifted.

When we can stay in this calm place despite the circumstances that present themselves, things can be worked through even when the answers are not apparent. As is said elsewhere in the book, "No problem can be solved from the same level of consciousness that created it" (Albert Einstein).

Authenticity is key

"People don't care what you know, until they know that you care."
Dr. William Pettit, psychiatrist, USA

Lao-tzu said, "The snow goose need not bathe to make itself white. Neither need you do anything but be yourself." It is our deep commitment to the truth of our "being-ness" that allows us to be our authentic selves.

We need to be ourselves and be respectful of both our sacred inheritance and that in others. We don't have to always be right; we just have to be human and do our jobs knowing that everyone is doing their best. If we don't know the answer, we can say so. People enjoy working with someone who is honest and has integrity. It makes a person authentic and approachable.

We need to be clear and explicit and speak with one voice: tell the same truth to every person, without judgment, and in as loving a way as we can. While not everyone will agree with what has been said, we will never have to worry if we stand in integrity and speak the truth as we see it and feel it. As the great William Shakespeare wrote, "This above all, to thine own self be true, And it must follow, as the night the day, Thou canst not then be false to any man."

I recall a time when there was an enormous battle going on between educators and the government. Circumstances found me squaring off in a public debate with the government representative for our region. Each of us stood in our truth and spoke respectfully to one another as we stated our positions in a myriad of ways. Despite our polar-opposite differences, neither of us resorted to name-calling or put-downs as is often seen in political debates.

At the end of the evening, the government official came to me, gave me a big hug, and said, "I don't believe a single word that came out of your mouth about the position you have taken. In fact, I believe you are dead wrong! However, I honor your honesty and integrity and thank you for standing in your truth. I believe that we can honestly and honorably agree to disagree."

This debate began an amazing dialogue that lasted the entire time this official was in office. He listened to my opinions, I listened to his, and together we found mutually satisfactory ways to deal with the issues that came along. We weren't always in agreement, but we did find common ground.

When it is necessary to speak to a particular issue, it is important to see it as just that, an issue, and then deal with it as an issue, minus the emotion. It is amazing how many problems can be solved easily when they are diffused and strong emotion is removed from the situation.

We have the opportunity to create a true community in our schools when we include others in the decision making, when we speak from our highest place, and when we do it with respect and love. Operating from a place of neutrality, where we accept the counsel of the school community, creates a sense of "we are all in it for the kids." The culture of the school becomes more positive when inclusiveness dissolves the barriers.

Working in neutral is honest, has integrity, and is efficacious. It is authentic and clean and puts our words into action. When someone says, "I hear what you are saying, but I am going to watch how your feet move," they will see the congruency of intention, thought, word, and action.

Be willing to change your mind

"No problem can be solved from the same level of consciousness that created it. We must learn to see the world anew."
Albert Einstein, German-born theoretical physicist

The world is never black and white—it is always shades of gray. Anyone who doesn't believe that is fooling herself!

Schools and similar institutions are often places where people arrive with a mind-set of how things "should" be and find themselves shocked when they are different. Some years ago, an alternative school was being established, and I was asked to be the principal. This public school's goal was to facilitate a crossover between homeschooling and public school. There were to be alternative timetables and parents as teachers; flexibility was to be the norm rather than the exception.

While flexibility can be the grease that makes the wheels turn, we discovered that every single person came to this alternative school with a different idea of what "alternative" meant. Black and white **did** exist— black and white times every single family enrolled and sometimes even between two parents! There was not a shade of gray in sight!

The philosophy of the school was that the parents would run it with the administrator operating as facilitator within the boundaries of the Ministry of Education. This school was the smallest one I had administered but with the largest number of problems I have ever encountered in all my years of school put together.

To me, "alternative" meant flexible. To some of the parents, it meant "my way or the highway!" After wishing I had never, ever taken on this challenge, I was reminded to look for the thread of essence. It was here too—just buried in the overwhelming demands of a few.

Over the course of the year, a couple of people who were unable to soften their beliefs left, while the rest of the parents began to build rapport through potlucks, sitting in a circle and learning to put their own stories on hold while listening deeply to others. By the end of the ten months, we had created a philosophy that we could all live with, a respect for our "grayness," and a commitment to listen more and talk less. As a community we moved away from being gripped in the same old way of seeing the world.

When we allowed ourselves to be flexible and to see the world from a range of viewpoints, we saw life at work. When we saw ourselves go up and down and up and down, we were able to take ourselves and others far less seriously.

Going through changes in levels of consciousness ourselves, we gained firsthand knowledge of what happens with every living soul in the world. When we experience it and allow ourselves to change our minds accordingly, we know that others can become "unstuck" and see the world from a new viewing space.

New space, new thoughts, and new reality: mind, thought, and consciousness in action.

Sometimes we get caught up in thinking that our point of view is the only one that is right and we are going to hold onto it come what may. Danger zone!

Sticking to our singular point of view is what a colleague calls a "cognitive love story." Translation? It means we fall in love with our own thinking and we refuse to change our minds. Think of the debates that can happen when people are positional in their thinking, that "my way or the highway" attitude!

Leaving our "cognitive love stories" in a parking lot and moving to a more neutral place allows us to be open to new and creative solutions to even age-old dilemmas. As Geoffrey Madon said, "The dust of exploded beliefs may make a fine sunset." Let's watch for those beautiful new hues in our schools!

Allow each day to begin fresh and new

"We do not step twice in the same river."
Heraclitus, pre-Socratic Greek philosopher

It is important to look at everyone as a tabula rasa. Each day is a new day, a new beginning. That does not mean that people aren't held to account for their actions. Instead, it means that consideration is given as to how to deal with the situation in a non judgmental way.

Some of us work in towns and villages that have seen generations come through the school system. I have heard teachers say, "Is she as musical as her brother? We'll be expecting great things!" That is a huge burden to bear if you simply want to be yourself with your own talents and contributions.

Often in relationships we inadvertently bring up the past and say, "I remember when you…" When this is a positive memory it can be lovely, but when it is not, it can buttonhole a person in a place that they have long since passed. Syd Banks said, "Negative memories and feelings are like scratches on your spectacles. They obscure your vision!"

When we are able to be open to the person the next time we meet, without the hangover of the thoughts and feelings of the day before, we can leave the past behind to live in the spirit of forgiveness. As Spittle and Mills write in their book *Wisdom from Within*, "People don't change because they are wrong. People change because they discover their health."

Each moment is brand-new—it is all that exists. In that very second, a person can begin fresh and can "jump the boundaries of time," as Sydney Banks would say. The person can change and manifest a new level of consciousness far beyond what he has left behind.

It is a privilege to see each individual "in the moment," to see her fresh and new and to allow her potential to bloom. This is an acknowledgement of her innate wisdom and the ability to change from within. This takes trust, and it creates permanent rather than transitory change.

Enjoy!

"People are at their most mindful when they are at play. If we find ways of enjoying our work, blurring the lines between work and play, the gains will be greater."
Ellen Langer, professor of psychology

Walking into a class of kindergarten children, one sees unbridled joy when the children are observed at play. Our work can be our play, and we can spend our days in joyful activity that helps to minimize the stress.

This century's research into the brain and its ability to learn shows that the brain seeks pleasure and that it learns best when it is in a joyful state. What a great way to justify increasing test scores while having fun practicing our craft!

A high school–aged friend was involved in a recent activity that pointed out this element in spades. Her teacher asked the students to do a "show and tell." These teenagers laughed uproariously—this was an activity that they had done in their primary days, but in secondary school? How could this be sound educational practice?

This brilliant teacher, gifted with creativity and a sound knowledge of the curriculum, had the students work to eleventh-grade goals about public speaking, preparation of an appropriate topic, delivering a message, and fully engaging an audience in a three-minute time period. The teacher created an enjoyable activity that hooked his adolescent students at the end of term and allowed them to show anything they wished. My young friend went off to school with her cat in a crate, something she had last done in kindergarten.

Laughter, joy, public speaking, learning about each other's private lives in an acceptable way—on and on the list could go out of a simple yet very sound lesson.

Will the students remember this day? You bet. Will they know something about one another that they can treasure? Absolutely. Was there an atmosphere of respect and engagement? Totally.

Laughter is one of the easiest ways to get to a neutral place of non judgment. It leaves us open to hear our inner wisdom, be open to that of others and to be present in the moment.

We can make our teaching thoughtful and earnest without making it sober. Warren Bennis says, "There are many ways of being creative. One can sing and dance. Or, one can create an environment in which singers and dancers flourish."

Let's find ways to allow people to flourish—to laugh, dance, sing, and enjoy learning and working.

~ 2 ~
There are no "throwaway" people.

Believe that every person wants and has the capacity to learn

"In every child who is born, under no matter what circumstances, and no matter what parents, the potentiality of the human race is born again."
James Agee & Walker Evans, American writer and photographer, Dust Bowl era

Over the years I have watched as teachers, administrators, and, on occasion, parents have seen only the "can't do" in a child.

James, an eight-year-old, had a December birthday and was such a young chap, emotionally and socially young. Playing with trucks was what he enjoyed, and had his parents and the school recognized that this was truly where he was at developmentally, he may have been saved a lot of grief. Instead, he was placed in kindergarten at four years and eight months and he struggled to make sense of this "cage" he was sentenced to for three hours every day.

James was a kid who should have been in the sandbox creating structures from sand and playing with Tonka toys. Instead, he was put in a no-win situation, having to sit still when he wasn't ready and being expected to be in a place he wasn't developmentally prepared to engage with.

James moved on to grade one after an unsuccessful kindergarten year, and at the end of term, his teacher said, "This child needs to do another year of first grade." James's parents knew that their child was beginning to feel the effects of this: he was quiet, withdrawn, and starting to feel badly about himself and exhibit negative tendencies.

James' parents decided to move to a different town and give him a new start. They felt that perhaps being with a new group of friends he wouldn't really notice that he was repeating grade one. But notice he did.

By the end of his second year in first grade he still wasn't reading, and his self-esteem had plummeted.

When he entered second grade, James' mother began to take some action. She worked with him each night trying to help him with his beginning reading skills, but he just said, "I can't. I don't know how. I'm dumb." Then would proceed to sob his little heart out. Recognizing the terrible state that her child was in, Mom resorted to "trickery," a strategy that was well intentioned and that she hoped would take her son beyond the negativity he was experiencing.

Mom discovered something that James wanted badly—a special costume for Halloween. He was so in love with this particular costume that she felt he would move past any barrier to get it. So they struck a deal: he would spend his evenings learning to read *Green Eggs and Ham* and she would spend her evenings listening to him while she created his costume. The passion in this little fellow's heart surpassed his fear and negative self-talk. Within a couple of weeks he had mastered the book, and his costume was ready for him when Halloween night came.

What was the difference? James had moved from "I can't" to "I can," and it shifted his reality.

James was fortunate—his mother didn't give up on him nor did one of the school counselors. Without these two steadfast and wise people, James may never have found his place of confidence, that place where he knew he could.

Like James, every single person has within them the capacity to learn and grow and to discover that "Yes, I can" feeling.

As educators, our basic premise and understanding needs to be this: that we never give up on a single person, be they student, teacher, or parent. While each of us evolves in different ways and at our own particular speed, every person moves along the continuum of growth. Sometimes the speed is so miniscule it is indiscernible, while at other times we seem to move at warp speed and change monumentally in an instant.

As educators we need to commit ourselves to recognizing that inside each individual is a place of innate wisdom that provides us with our "savvy" or common sense. This place of intuition is one that we need to learn to listen to and trust. It is our compass for life.

As the world becomes a busier place filled with social networking and the constancy of contact, heads are filled with thoughts, and instant reaction is expected and demanded. While this technology is going to stay and can have amazing benefits, it is important that we recognize and help others to see that the way to recognize the call of this inner compass is through a quiet mind.

As educators shift their thinking to see students as whole and not broken, the future will be more hopeful. They will commit to assisting students to discover the inner knowing that helps them to believe they CAN succeed.

Evidence for this type of success can be found in the long-term studies done in the Kauai resilience project. This study has shown that people can and do flourish over time despite the background they come from or the odds that are stacked against them. Each and every person wants and has the capacity to learn.

It is important that we remember this: there are no "throwaway" people—none—only potential in disguise. We are here to notice and acknowledge the capacity in each person. That is our number one job in schools.

Seeing all students "at promise" rather than "at risk" takes us to a world of infinite possibility!

There are no "throwaway" people.

Create opportunities for all voices to be heard

"There is a longing among all people and creatures to have a sense of purpose and worth. To satisfy that common longing in all of us we must respect each other."
Chief Dan George, chief of the Tsleil-Waututh Nation, Canada

When we set up opportunities for all voices to be heard, a chance for strong community commitment occurs.

I have observed schools where this has been provided for even the youngest students. This has expanded outward to include the community seniors, and the results have been phenomenal.

OUR school is all that is ever heard in such places. It is never MY school, but our school. This collective feeling creates a powerful sense of community.

This sense of a superordinate goal from the collection of voices contains so much energy, love, and power that it becomes almost sacred.

Since the days of Socrates, schools have been in existence to teach children how to be worthy, contributing citizens. How can they learn this most effectively? By living it! We need to give them opportunities to be active participants, sharing their voices and their ideas. It is life in action.

A father, new to our community, brought this point home to me. George arrived at my office door one morning and expressed surprise that there wasn't more opportunity for input from parents and students. His family had moved to our town from a large city where their children's school had a population of two thousand. George found our model for involvement very "top down" with no real room for making a difference. We saw ourselves as friendly and inclusive, so his observations came as a bit of a surprise!

George was invited to give a presentation on the way his children's school had been run. He described a circle, one where even in a school of two thousand all voices were considered, all opinions were listened to, and consensus was reached on important decisions.

Intrigued, we decided to implement his suggestions. We tried a variety of ways to accomplish what George had told us and finally found one that worked for us: a combination of family-grouped, small meetings that brought decisions to the whole school meetings where we were able to come to consensus.

Most interesting was how this same circle was used to effect change in how we conducted our staff meetings. If a decision was "on my neck," then the staff agreed that I could make what we called an "Austocratic" decision, but there weren't many of those. All others were brought to the circle of staff and parent representatives, and we came to consensus on all decisions that did not have to be held in confidence.

George introduced us to the concept of a circle of trust, long used for consultation by aboriginal peoples and by different religious groups. What we discovered is that it works in public institutions as well.

We have seen small children learn to bring their ideas forward in a whole school meeting, ideas that have changed the policies by which the school has been run. In an atmosphere of respect and trust, these little people can be as connected to their innate wisdom as those who are many years their senior—sometimes even more!

When we offer students, staff, and parents opportunities to have a voice and truly listen in authentic and meaningful ways, the results are astounding.

Class meetings, whole school meetings, family groupings, and pods are all ways that every student's voice can be heard. Similar consensual meeting styles are valuable in soliciting parental and staff insights.

All we need be is open, flexible, respectful, willing to share responsibility, and willing to listen deeply.

Ask questions and listen deeply to the answers

"To 'listen' another's soul into a condition of disclosure and discovery may be almost the greatest service any human being ever performs for another."
Douglas V. Steere, American Quaker ecumenist

We can't ever presume to know where people are coming from because we all live in separate realities created by our personal thinking. In our innocence, we often make assumptions and act according to those assumptions.

Yet when we come from a place of detachment, a place free from judgment, we can ask genuine and respectful questions that will help us to understand our colleagues, the students, and their parents in a more authentic and honest way. Our eyes are open to finding the places where we can provide support in appropriate ways.

Linda Kavelin Popov, one of the founders of the Virtues Project, has a wonderful word that she uses for this way of being with another: she calls it "companioning." Linda says that companioning requires deep listening, is most effective when we don't have an agenda, is not meant to fix but to support, consists mostly of silence and open-ended questions, and requires trust.

I learned from Linda that if I used "what" and "how" questions rather than "why" questions, we would get to the heart of the matter more quickly. She also taught me that after getting to the heart of the issue, it was a good time to ask a question that would reflect on something such as a virtue that might help the person sharing to move forward.

It has been my experience that listening deeply to another's perceptions helps us to stay open to a world of possibilities rather than bounded by the restrictions of past thoughts. It is so easy to paint a person with a particular brush from our past experiences with them, but when we can stay open and allow newness to come in, we can have fresh starts all the time.

When we remember to see the innocence in everyone, it helps us to hear their answers from a place of love and respectful caring; it offers the gift of acceptance. As Syd Banks said, "humility isn't thinking less of yourself, it is thinking of yourself less." When we feel accepted, we let go of the arsenal of thoughts we hold to defend ourselves. When that drops, newness and possibility appear.

There are no "throwaway" people.

Look for the innate strengths in the community of learners

"What is a weed? A plant whose virtues have never been discovered."
Ralph Waldo Emerson, American essayist, lecturer, and poet

Every community of learners has talents and strengths to honor and celebrate. When we acknowledge and honor the gifts in each individual, we are recognizing their unique spirits. Instead of a plain old buffet, we have a virtual feast!

As educators, our job is to find our student's magic spot, the inner place he or she loves to be. Passion is the fire in the belly—the expression of who we are meant to be in life. Knowing this, honoring it, and allowing passion to be expressed, we pay the deepest of respect to people.

I once worked in a school that welcomed parents to come in and share their areas of passion. This was an amazing experience. As a generalist, I had some talent in music and the academic areas of the curriculum, but when it came to visual arts or physical education, I had a failing grade!

Welcoming in those who had passion and creative talent in my weaker areas could have taken me in one direction or another. On one hand, I could have felt diminished and embarrassed to admit that I was not an expert at everything, or I could instead celebrate the fact that parents with those talents were willing to share their time in my class. Fortunately, I opted for the latter.

I learned to make natural dyes from things in the garden. Onionskins boiled down make a beautiful color. How would I ever have known unless I, too, put myself in the place of being a learner and checking it out with an expert?

I learned how to make excellent vegetarian dishes, not a skill I had learned growing up on a farm or being married to a meat-and-potatoes man! Capture the flag, how to throw a ball properly, and new dance steps—all put me in the learner's seat. And the greatest thing of all? Students got to see two things:

1. Adults can be lifelong learners—you never know all there is to know.

2. Every person has his or her own strengths to offer.

Some educational environments do not have the community talent to draw upon that our schools did. However, within a staff there are a variety of strengths and talents, and with flexibility and cooperation, people can trade off time with one another and teach in their areas of passion. It might be one art lesson on how to paint portraits, or teaching how to do the long jump in physical education, or it may extend to an entire term or year. Whatever it is, being adaptable and flexible in playing to the strengths and passions of the people on the team builds on the expertise in your school.

We each have our own facets of passion. Polished in a positive and passionate way, we get the perfectly cut diamond. When we polish each other's stars of passion we all shine brightly and it brings an end to the competition to be the brightest star. Instead, we honor the strengths and talents in each other.

It quickly becomes evident that when every person's area of strength is acknowledged as having equal value, there is unbridled vibrancy in the building!

There are no "throwaway" people.

Stay in the flow

"The quality of the imagination is to flow and not to freeze."
Ralph Waldo Emerson, American essayist, lecturer, and poet

When we are in that space where we have lost all track of time and experience a sense of total ease with what we are doing, we are said to be "in the flow." Our day feels as though it is timeless and we are totally in the moment. In this state of flow, we are able to accomplish so much more because our minds aren't as cluttered or preoccupied.

Martha Kaufeldt (*Begin with the Brain: Orchestrating the Learner Centered Classroom, Corwin Press 2009*) describes flow as "an optimal experience when people report feelings of deep concentration and enjoyment…a state that is so completely focused it amounts to absolute absorption in an activity…the mind and body are in complete harmony."

When we organize schools to allow people choice and to share personal passion, amazing things happen. When I was first learning about how to work with the feeling of flow, one day a week was devoted to project learning and allowing students to work in their areas of passion. This was orchestrated in terms of modality, choice, and interest, and it also had purpose, goals, and task completion developed with each student.

Creating these longer spaces in time that allowed for total engagement in the learning process was amazing. I found that classroom management issues disappeared on those days. Curiosity in each other's projects created an atmosphere of authentic sharing, and the range of creativity was exhilarating for everyone involved.

As we set up schools and classrooms, we need to be aware that our students, as well as the staff, need the opportunity to experience flow. We need to find ways to design our programs so that students are given the chance to "get lost" in a project and to feel their own insights emerge as they tinker with ideas and projects.

All of us know what it feels like to get so lost in time that we forget to look at our watches. We are captured by the moment and the ease of what we are doing, and before we know it, the day has slipped by and much has been accomplished.

We don't need to worry about the goals that will be met. When we trust that this kind of immersion has value, it will be obvious that learning has taken place. It may happen in a more convoluted way than with a more linear process, and the reporting of it may be more difficult to fit into a computerized box that acknowledges a goal being met, but learning *will* have taken place and at a deeper and more thoughtful level. Critical thinking skills, so difficult to plan and teach, will have been met, and students will have had a most enjoyable and authentic learning experience.

And for the teachers? There will be a day of facilitating learning and doing what education truly means: to draw out.

Schools are where we can learn to be "in service" to others

"The best way to find yourself is to lose yourself in service to others."
Mahatma Gandhi, Indian nationalist leader practicing nonviolence

Often in schools we are preoccupied with finding the latest "in-service" where we can get more. The focus can be flipped to being "in service" to our communities and to give rather than get. We are there to serve the needs of our students—that is why schools exist.

All the world's sacred texts have this tenet of service as the "golden rule" underpinning their credos: love, respect, and understanding for those around us. These virtues awaken us to compassion and empathy for others. As we allow our understanding to deepen and open our eyes for opportunities to share these feelings with one another, students and staff awaken to deeper feelings in themselves. It is this inner awakening that enlivens and enriches our experiences in life.

There are countless ways that teachers accomplish this in their classrooms. I know one teacher who takes her students to a local nursing home each week. Out of respect for the "come from" of these very elderly and demented patients, Irene has taught the children songs that resonate with their audience. She had an initial parent meeting and explained why the songs the children were learning were from the past and might raise a few eyebrows. Once the parents understood the purpose, Irene had total parental support.

Another example is the service work done by matching secondary students with the residents in a senior citizen home. These budding friendships have provided powerful ways to connect generations; in fact, it has become the name of the project: *Connecting Generations*!

Student service in the area of stewardship of the environment is another major contributor to lifelong learning and caring for mother earth. Teachers working with their students on salmon enhancement projects, cleaning the beaches, and planting gardens and trees all provide opportunities for both students and staff to be in service to a world beyond themselves.

When students, staff, and parents experience a feeling of belonging and acceptance, of respect and love in their school community, an opening is created for sharing this same feeling with those they touch in the broader community and the world. When people reach out to share, there is an upsurge of gratitude.

There are no "throwaway" people.

Share the leadership

"The wicked leader is he who the people despise. The good leader is he who the people revere. The great leader is he who the people say, 'We did it ourselves.'"
Lao-tzu, ancient Chinese philosopher

Blurring the lines and sharing the running of an organization creates an empowering culture. People feel a sense of ownership and come to trust that what they contribute will make a difference to the greater good.

Sharing the leadership eliminates competition and allows people to both contribute and listen from a place of trust. Acknowledging that an infinite source of wisdom is within each person creates a sense of oneness and wholeness that encircles the school community. As the saying goes, "A rising tide lifts all boats."

We are all leaders in various ways because we all have strengths to share. It takes a lot of trust the first few times you let go of the reins, but it pays off well.

I have had the privilege of working on staffs and committees where a multitude of ideas have been generated that call for specific expertise and lots of "elbow grease." Hands go up, people volunteer to take on areas they feel comfortable with, and by the end of an organizational meeting there is ownership and excitement in the air.

It can happen for a year's school-growth plan, a professional development plan, a concert, a student yearbook—you name it—sharing the leadership with staff, parents, and students can be an exhilarating and exciting adventure.

Flattening the hierarchy to include staff, students, parents, and the greater community creates an opportunity for all the participants to offer opinions, but more importantly, to share passions. Administrators can look for the strengths in the people they are charged to lead and uncover opportunities for them to share their understandings. Creating opportunities for accessing these capacities provides everyone a way to share their gifts, to contribute, and to be in service.

When people feel that they are contributing, they feel ownership; when they feel ownership, they provide service above and beyond the call because they are connected in a very deep way with the enterprise. When one has "bought in" because he or she has been welcomed to do so, the outpouring and service that is offered is pure and powerful.

Students, staff, and parents all have the inner capacity to be leaders. When we provide a multiplicity of opportunities by trusting the power of the essential curriculum, innate intelligence has the sacred ground on which to plant seeds.

~ 3 ~

The essence of success lies in nurturing positive, genuine feelings and recognizing the virtues in one another.

Let trust, respect, and rapport be the cornerstones of your foundation

"We trust others to do what they say they will do and give them the space to be trustworthy."
Dr. Dan Popov, Linda Kavelin Popov, & John Kavelin,
founders of the Virtues Project

The ideas are repeated over and over again in this little book: trust and non judgment are pivotal to developing rapport and relationship.

When we have the opportunity to learn and work in a culture where trust, respect, and rapport form the foundation, we can soar. These qualities become givens, and people do not have to worry or question what will happen. They know they are safe. They know they can be who they are. They know that they will be respected.

One incident that readily comes to mind is the student who carried her lunch to school in a camera case. This youngster was in the sixth grade, and I always thought it courageous of her to dare to be different. Within her school community she was treated with the deepest of respect because she had developed rapport and felt trust in the environment.

Unfortunately, this same young woman had to catch a bus to her home that had students from other schools on it. Not part of the student body where a trusting environment had been fostered, this child suffered miserably and ended up crying nightly. She loved her camera case and wanted to bring her lunch in it. Why? It had been her mother's and she had died not long before.

Eventually her classmates were able to help her find a solution. She would carry her camera case in a larger pack and none of the bullies on the bus would be suspicious. When it was time to eat her lunch, she eagerly took out her special camera case lunch kit, spread out her food, and felt her mother's presence with her. Her friends listened, they were trustworthy, and they allowed this youngster to deal with her needs in her own way.

How do we develop rapport? By listening to what people have to say. From the youngest child bringing in the snakeskin she found in the field, to the angry parent who is overwrought with frustration: listen, listen, and listen some more.

We can allow the person we are sharing time with to be the most important thing in that moment. Let him be the focus, enjoy him, set him at ease, and find ways to exchange in honest dialogue.

Above all, it is important to see others' innocence and recognize that we all possess the same innate intelligence. We are all the same. There is no "they," only "us."

Being consciously aware of our personal perspective in any given moment lessens judgment and blame and takes us back to a neutral place where we can listen with openness and be reflective and support- ive. Our conscious awareness becomes the great equalizer and stabilizer.

A community of learners is built on relationship, relationship, relationship

"One of the marvelous things about community is that it enables us to welcome and help people in a way we couldn't as individuals. When we pool our strength and share the work and responsibility, we can welcome many people, even those in deep distress, and perhaps help them find self-confidence and inner healing."
Jean Vanier, Canadian humanist, philosopher, and theologian

A new school was to be built, and several of us chose to be part of the inaugural staff. We knew that it would be a challenge being in a small country school, but our excitement about the world of new possibilities triumphed over our fears.

We knew that building community would help us to be cohesive and strong, but we had no inkling of how very powerful it would be.

Today, students and parents come up to the original staff and talk about the magical days, the days where we dared to dream big ideas, where children were amused by their own creativity and imagination on the playground, where the common thread was respect and caring.

This was the thread of essence, the essential curriculum, the one we based that school upon. We built community, and because it was so incredibly strong, we were able to face the joys of each and every success and the devastation of sorrow from the death of a child within the same circle of caring. A strong, supportive, loving, and respectful community is the result of teaching the essential curriculum. Through it, we learn to help each other and create a circle of shared power.

When we embed our teaching and school culture with healthy relationships, we create more time to focus on academic learning.

When we begin to recognize that we are responsible for our own thoughts, it lessens the blame game. When this element is taken out of the community, it reverses the responsibility and places it with its owner. Miraculously, it changes things immensely. The culture changes from a model of "power over" to one of "power with" those in the school community.

This creates a more peaceful and positive culture for the students, and it frees the teachers to teach rather than manage behavior. It provides principals with the opportunity to support their staffs rather than have to constantly spend time dealing with disciplinary difficulties.

Over the years I have watched young people accept growing responsibility for who they are in the world. Creating a community of learners where all are encouraged, taught, and expected to be accountable for their actions in a nonthreatening environment makes a tremendous difference in school cultures. The students become leaders, mentors, and excellent role models. Bullying then becomes virtually nonexistent and violent acts cease, making schools safe and secure places for students to be.

When we are in relationship with others, we support and care about them. When we care, we are less likely to use our power over others and will be more collaborative and supportive.

In a more natural, open, and honest way, people can enjoy being in relationship in this community of learners and are willing to problem solve and grow. It is a venue that provides everyone with a voice in what counts. When you are for it, you can't be against it! This atmosphere of sharing creates a safe haven that enriches all its members.

The health of the staff is paramount

*"To put the world right... we must first cultivate our personal life;
we must first set our hearts right."*
Confucius, Chinese teacher and philosopher

One of the interesting tasks I have undertaken in my career has been to do professional development in other parts of the country. I was called into a school in another province, and the goal was to "help to get the staff on the same page." A broad statement of need indeed, and my request for more details resulted in vague responses such as "they don't all see things the same way, some are very linear while others are more global in their viewpoint of curriculum." I was still left scratching my head even after probing for more answers.

I flew across the country and showed up ready to start the day's workshop. I walked up to the school and found the door locked up tight. I went to a different door. Same thing. I knew I had the right dates because I had confirmed everything the week before, so I was mystified. I knocked and knocked and eventually a custodian came and let me in. No welcoming committee. No administrator or professional development representative. Nothing. I was beginning to feel nervous.

The custodian was kind and led me to the office. After a cursory welcome, I was shown into the rooms we would be using. It was not set up, and when I inquired about this I was shown the storage room where I could find stacks of chairs. This was the most bizarre gig I had ever experienced! But it got even more intriguing. When the staff arrived for the start of the workshop, many were wearing sunglasses that they did not take off for the entire day. None of my group exercises like "turn to your neighbor and share..." worked. I got no feedback, and at the end of an exhausting day I left thinking I had totally bombed. But the feedback from the school was somewhere between neutral and positive, so I was bewildered.

Two months later I returned for the next workshop. This time the door was unlocked and the room set up. The principal got up to welcome everyone and said, "Well, I am so pleased that after so many years we are all speaking to one another." Alarm bells rang in my head, and as I got up to speak I leaned forward and quietly said to the principal, "We need to talk at the break. I think there are things you need to tell me."

My discussion with the principal gave evidence of a very unhealthy staff relationship. People hadn't spoken to each other in many years after a major disagreement on policy. The achievement levels in the school had suffered, and the parents dreaded sending their children to this school, many opting, instead, for a private school. It was the clearest example I have ever experienced of the impact that an unhealthy staff has on students' learning.

The happy news is that some people with influence knew that the culture had to change, and they were prepared to do all they could to try to alter it. After a few months, the staff had regained its health and was working as a team. The students were reaping the benefits in many ways. Parents were happy to send their kids to school, the staff was enjoying coming to work, and best of all, the students were learning in a positive and optimistic environment.

The health of the helpers is immensely important. This holds true for the entire staff. A healthy viewpoint generates a hopeful attitude that honors and acknowledges the best of those in our care.

When we honor everyone by listening carefully and deeply, by making personal contact, and by showing interest in who and what the person is, we create feelings of trust and acceptance. Creating a space of warmth and caring provides a nurturing environment in which everyone develops to his or her fullest potential.

Listening to ourselves is as important as listening to others. We need to be aware of our own moods and feelings. When we are conscious of our thoughts and feelings, knowing that they create our reality, we recognize the power that we have within ourselves. The essential curriculum guides us yet again.

Conscious awareness helps us to see that from a relaxed and calm state of mind we create an environment where working and learning are engaging and interesting for everyone. And the magic of it? It takes no money, no time, no governmental policies—just conscious awareness of our own thoughts and feelings: personal responsibility.

Words can be powerful allies. They have the potential to support and enhance both our own inner growth and that of those around us in immeasurable ways. It is important to listen carefully to what is coming out of our mouths and to notice the impact it is having on our own thinking and on those around us.

When the entire staff is centered in health and able to see with clarity, it makes a huge impact on the atmosphere. Like ripples when a pebble drops in water, the staff has the capacity to radiate calm assurance. The opposite holds true when the staff is not in a healthy place. We are forever in charge of the choice.

The essence of success lies in nurturing positive, genuine feelings.

Rise above the nitty-gritty

"Our feelings are the barometer of the soul.
They are the measure of our thinking."
Sydney Banks, author, philosopher and theosophist

It is important that we remind ourselves not to get gripped by the details—they don't get us anywhere but lost! The details are in the world of form, and to find the way, we have to reverse our direction and see where it has been created. While it seems mysterious, it is at its core simplicity.

Focusing on the feeling in the school gives us a much better chance of being able to shift and change. The feeling is our touchstone, the automatic gift that lets us know where things sit. Instead of going through the complexity of analyzing what is formed in the details, we can skip to the simple method of checking the "feeling barometer"!

These kinds of questions help check out the school or classroom barometer:

- Is there calmness in the air?

- Are there kind and respectful feelings between the children?

- Are the adults being respectful of the students and each other?

- Are we walking our talk?

- Is there dignity in how we conduct ourselves?

- Is this a place people want to spend their days?

Notice, notice, notice, and notice some more.

I used to do a goofy thing each day—I would go out on the playground for a swing! It was a lovely way to casually interact with the students, to hear what they were saying to one another, and to observe the type of play that was going on. When in schools with older kids, I casually meandered about stopping to chat, was unobtrusive, and listened. Same thing in the staff room—the conversations in there can be revealing, and the temperature is very easy to read. Parking lots outside the school and the corner grocery store where parents are chatting all give hints as to how things are going.

When we are able to stay in a positive feeling, we are less gripped by needless details. Focusing on optimism and positivity is the fast track to change. When we stay out of the nitty-gritty and remain in that good feeling, the details are handled more efficiently and effectively!

The essential curriculum is in action, yet again.

Find feelings of gratitude and express them

"Gratitude paves the way."
Elsie Spittle, internationally recognized trainer and consultant

When we walk into our buildings and feel grateful for the opportunity to be in service to the staff, the students, and their families, we have achieved job satisfaction and contentment. This becomes contagious, and when we share our feelings of gratitude with others, we spread the feeling quicker than the chickenpox can spread in the same building!

The essential curriculum is the underpinning of this space—a sense of deep gratitude. Our feelings are our barometer; they are the gauges that tell us where our consciousness and thoughts are residing. The more gratitude we feel, the greater our sense of contentment. And when we feel that, we can't help but give it away.

When we stand at the door and greet the students and staff and are there at the end of the day to ask how the day went and to bid them farewell, we are giving the gift of interest and creating a sense of belonging. People are able to share the wonderful things that have happened during their day, be they students or staff. Taking the time to be available and allowing this expression to take place demonstrates the greatest of respect.

While mentoring student teachers for a nearby university, I had the occasion to be in a classroom of sixth-grade students. Each morning part of the regular classroom teacher's routine was to have a moment for the day's intentions. The leader of this changed weekly, just like the board monitors and cleanup people. A brilliant idea, it allowed every child to have practice leading just such a circle.

When it came time for sharing intentions for the day, there were a wide variety of things mentioned. The designated student got up and started the day by telling what he was grateful for and what his intentions were for the day. Some students talked about finishing projects, while others wanted to study for the upcoming spelling test. One thanked his friends for asking him if his mom got the new job she had applied for. A few students talked about social intentions such as helping the younger kids learn to throw a ball, but all were moments in time where the students were looking forward with a positive and optimistic attitude. It was very moving to observe these moments of warmth, kindness, and positive intentions.

When we say "thank you" for sincere and genuine good works, the recipient glows with the same feeling we have just extended. It becomes an electrical current that is unstoppable as long as attention is paid to it. We have plugged into the highest voltage one can give! How simple it is—no lengthy in-service, no expensive purchases, nothing complex, just a feeling of gratitude and caring that permeates the culture of the school. The message? Plug in! Let the essential curriculum be the energy source in your school.

Listen deeply

"One who cares, listens."
Paul Tillich, German American existentialist philosopher

Listening deeply creates a receptive environment, one where insights can be revealed. This is the pathway we are looking for—one where people discover the incredible wisdom and beauty that lies within.

When we listen to others from an open, neutral, and nonjudgmental place, it affords the person that is sharing an immediate opportunity to develop trust in the listener. A feeling of mutual warmth develops, and the two people find a place of rapport with one another. It is this act of "companioning" in a quiet and respectful way that allows the true spirit of each person to come forward. It allows vulnerability.

Often we enter a conversation holding our own assumptions about who a person is and what she has to say. Before the person even opens her mouth, we have a running commentary going on in our heads. If we aren't mindful, we miss the little clues that give us the most important next steps in developing a relationship or resolving an issue.

I have observed an amazing woman who I hold in the highest regard. On the surface Laura appears shy, very quiet, and not the kind of person who could make a difference. Her leadership skills are subtle yet powerful, and she accomplishes this through her ability to listen deeply and make connections.

One of the projects this woman has undertaken is to connect senior citizens with adolescents. Laura wanted to eliminate the barrier that sometimes exists between older people and loud, rambunctious teenagers. By engaging in conversations with the teens, observing them at school, and having visits over tea with the seniors, Laura was able to match up the perfect pairs of people. Matching a war vet with a young man who was studying history, coupling a canoe builder with a lad interested in wood-working, and pairing an accomplished, award-winning nurse with a bud-ding nurse practitioner, Laura paved the way to letting go of assumptions about age difference and created a place where young and old could see each other as people. These friendships have lasted through time, enhanc-ing the lives of both ends of the age continuum. Laura's ability to listen deeply has created joy for teens and seniors alike.

Listening from a place of detachment lets us see the other person's "come from." This doesn't mean that the listener needs to commiserate or to "fix" something, rather it gives the opportunity to discern the other person's point of view and what underlies it.

Often when a person needs to talk, he finds his answers simply by listening to his own voice. The listener doesn't provide the answers. The listener's task is simply to provide the space for the speaker's wisdom to emerge, to be his companion, and when appropriate, ask questions.

Sometimes when listening to someone, we may notice ourselves be-ginning to judge or to say "yes but." This is a little signal to be quiet and slip back into neutral and truly be a listener. This is what Laura was able to teach her students through the experience of being with a senior. They learned to share their very different "come froms" with each other, and I dare say, the seniors learned more about it themselves.

Students, parents, and staff find their way by being powerful lis-teners. It has been my experience that when the staff has modeled and helped students learn to listen to each other, they have come up with amazing solutions to behaviors that appeared to be entrenched. The same has happened with parents and staff members. Everyone wants to be heard, truly heard. When we provide the space for that to happen, it allows sanity to prevail.

When we are able to listen in this deep way, we are more aware of in-sights from our own inner wisdom. When we allow this beautiful space to be present, we become true companions and lay the ground for the thinking and perception of the person speaking to shift.

Love them all

"Love is a feeling that comes in many disguises. It may be caring for someone in need, loving your husband, loving your children, caring for and helping your neighbors and friends. Or it may be bringing a little joy to others who are less fortunate. There is no end to the different ways to use this beautiful gift called love."
Sydney Banks, author, philosopher and theosophist

When we choose to see the members of our learning community from a neutral, non judgmental place, we give the greatest gift we can give. This is the vehicle that allows unconditional love to flow between people.

Our schools deserve to be filled with love and joy so that the legacy we leave our children is the opportunity to be immersed in this feeling of true acceptance and respect. The essential curriculum is there to be shared. It is our students' birthright and our responsibility to ensure that it has the opportunity to be uncovered.

Conclusion

Students, staff, and parents cannot help but be touched by the positive benefits of being in environments where love and joy are permitted to be the "feeling barometer" and the essential curriculum forms the foundation.

This essential curriculum has helped people to uncover their place of creativity, wisdom, and compassion. It can sustain a person for life, and while at times it may seem hidden like the sun behind a cloud, it prevails.

When the foundation stones are the essential curriculum—one built on virtues of trust and love, one that acknowledges and invites all learners to entertain the wonder and awe of learning and engages them as full participants—it can be seen and felt as soon as you walk in the door of the building. The first encounter will tell you instantly whether it is a place of safety and caring, one that honors and nurtures people in all ways.

Ever hopeful in the pursuit of positive outcomes, people continue to look for something that will create sustainable change. I believe that the essential curriculum is that ingredient.

Consciously realizing that we have the ability to think and the power to view the world in new ways can become a catalyst for lifelong change. Seeing it in action in schools is a powerful motivator to help us continue looking forward with optimism.

Explicitly teaching and using the positive language of virtues brings uplifting language into schools. This language of caring and love, hope and joy, helpfulness and service begins to flow naturally in these settings.

We *can* change schools! They can be successful, and all of the individuals within them can be productive if we open the door to something new. It is all about the feeling: the abiding culture. As Peter Drucker is reported to have said, "Culture eats strategy for breakfast!" And so the feelings are foundational to the authenticity of the strategies.

This exciting task can be undertaken. It requires people to open their minds to something different—quieter, open minds—ones where individuals are willing to let go of "being right" and put aside the urge to say, "We've done this before—it didn't work," or "This sounds like the sixties."

The essential curriculum holds the message of true self-esteem, empowerment, and resiliency: to simply know from inside "I can, I will, I know." It creates school communities where students develop in their wholeness—academically, emotionally, artistically, physically, socially, and in moral character. It unfetters thoughts and frees people to live stable and secure lives, in service of others.

Believe that change is possible. Know that a change in consciousness leads to a change in thinking and subsequently to a change in reality. In a loving, caring, and compassionate environment filled with virtuous and positive feelings, people grow and flourish. In such a place there are no throwaway people, only potential in a variety of disguises.

Consider opening yourself to a new way of viewing education. Think how incredible it will be to offer young people safe havens in which to be truly successful human beings.

The time is now.

The solution is here.

People are waiting.

The world needs this hope.

May you find love and joy in your work with others.

Barb Aust

Awakening Schools

British Columbia, Canada

www.awakeningschools.com

June 2013

Source Materials

The underpinnings of the essential curriculum are to be found in Sydney Banks' teachings on the Three Principles of Mind, Thought, and Consciousness. Michael Neill, internationally renowned transformational coach, radio show host, and bestselling author shared a summary from a talk Syd gave. This summary can be found in Michael's latest book. *(The Inside-Out Revolution, Hay House 2013)*

Syd Banks said:

"What are Mind, Consciousness, and Thought?

Mind is the intelligence of all things; Consciousness makes you aware; and Thought is like the rudder of a ship. It guides you through life, and if you learn to use that rudder properly, you can guide your way through life far better than you ever imagined. You can go from one reality to another. You can find your happiness and when illusionary sadness comes from memories, you don't try to figure it out. Please don't try to do that – you'll get yourself in trouble. All you have to do is realize that it's Thought.

The second that you realize that it's Thought, you are touching the very essence of psychological experience. You're back to the 'now,' you're back to happiness. So don't get caught up on a lot of details...

And that's where life comes from: inside out. It's spiritual knowledge. It's there, everybody has it and people don't realize that. There's no human being more spiritual than you – everybody is equal.

And you know what the equality is?

That we all derive from Mind Consciousness, and Thought.

That's the equalizer."

Websites where you can learn more about The Three Principles are:

http://www.sydneybanks.org/

http://www.3pgc.org/

http://www.3phd.net.

Other helpful Three Principles materials for those working with youth are those by Ami Chen Mills (http://amichen.com/books-publications/).

While the materials are not specific to The Three Principles, those created by The Virtues Project may assist teachers to explicitly teach and use the positive language of virtues with young children. The project's website can be found at www.virtuesproject.com. Go to the section for educators and you will find materials that may be helpful in facilitating discussion with young people.

40034940R00037

Made in the USA
Charleston, SC
23 March 2015